Video Animation
and Photography

Anastasia Suen

Rourke
Educational Media

rourkeeducationalmedia.com

SUPPLIES TO COMPLETE ALL PROJECTS:

- Animoto login (ask an adult)
- cell phone or tablet
- computer
- fasteners (clips, clothes pins, safety pins, duct tape, etc)
- floor area to roll out green screen
- glue
- green cloth or roll of paper
- green screen app (ask an adult to download it)
- items to move (plastic figures, Lego, cutouts, clay)
- lights (four)
- paper
- pencil
- Pivot stick figure animation software (ask an adult to download it)
- scissors
- step stool or ladder
- stop-motion animation software (ask an adult to download it)
- tall object to hang green screen over (curtain, pole, shelf)
- tripod

Table of Contents

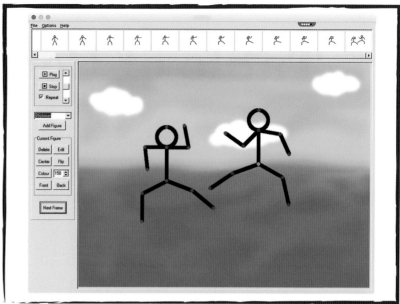

4

Video Animation and Photography

Film your family history as it happens. Create short videos with music. **Animate** a stick figure. Make a **stop-motion** movie. Add amazing backgrounds to your photos with a green screen app.

Record History

TAKE YOUR CAMERA TO A FAMILY EVENT AND RECORD HISTORY. MAKE A MOVIE LIKE THE PROS.

Here's How:

1. Turn your phone sideways. Now it looks like a TV screen.

2. Hold the camera with both hands. Keep your arms close to your body as you move the camera.

Tip:
If you film with your phone up and down, black bands will appear on both sides of the movie when you show it on another screen later.

3. Choose a live event to film. Record a game or a family event.

4. Begin your film with a wide view. Slowly look around with the camera.

5. Show the **location**, the place where the event is happening.

Tip:

Movie directors begin with a **long shot**. They show the location of the film. In a long shot, viewers can see the actors from head to toe.

Making Movie Magic

A camera needs light to film a scene. As you move around the location, remember to check the light.

If the brightest light is behind the people you are filming, they will block the light. It will be too dark for the camera.

Move to another place. Stand where the brightest light is behind you.

6. Move the camera closer. Walk over to the main event.

7. Film the action. Show people in motion.

Tip:

After viewers see the world of the story, the director shows the action with a **mid-shot**. The camera moves to the middle of the scene. Now only part of each actor's body is visible.

8. Now move the camera even closer. Film faces and the feelings they show.

9. Then move the camera back to the action.

10. Film the actions and the feelings until the event is over.

11. If possible, end the film with a feelings shot.

Tip:

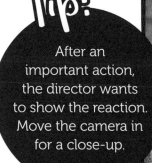

After an important action, the director wants to show the reaction. Move the camera in for a close-up.

YOU WILL NEED:

- computer
- Pivot stick figure animation software (ask an adult to download it)

Tip!

The free Pivot software download comes with other free software that may turn on the anti-virus program. You do not have to install the other software to use the animation program.

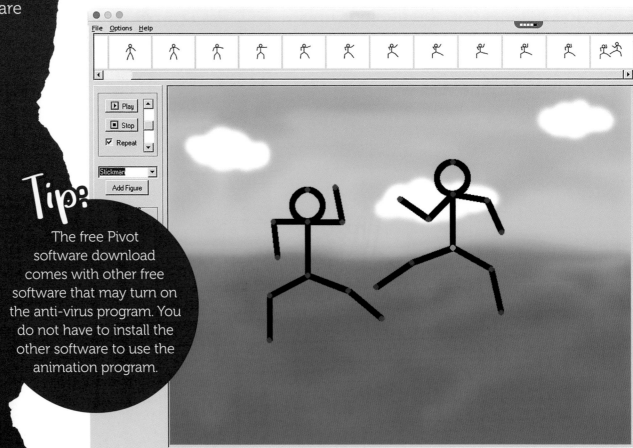

LEARN ANIMATION. MAKE A STICK FIGURE MOVE.

Here's How:

1. Open the Pivot program.

2. There will be a stick figure in the middle of the screen.

3. Click a red dot. The black lines will turn blue.

4. Drag the red dot to a new place.

5. The stick figure will move that body part.

Tip:
If you want to move the whole body to a different place on the screen, click and drag the orange dot.

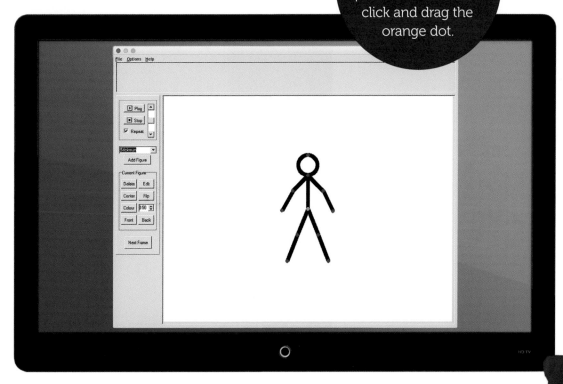

6. Press the *Next Frame* button to make a new frame.

7. Click another dot and drag it. Move the stick figure again.

8. Press the *Next Frame* button again.

9. Make ten frames.

10. Then click the *Play* button.

Tip: The frames you make will appear in the timeline at the top of the main window.

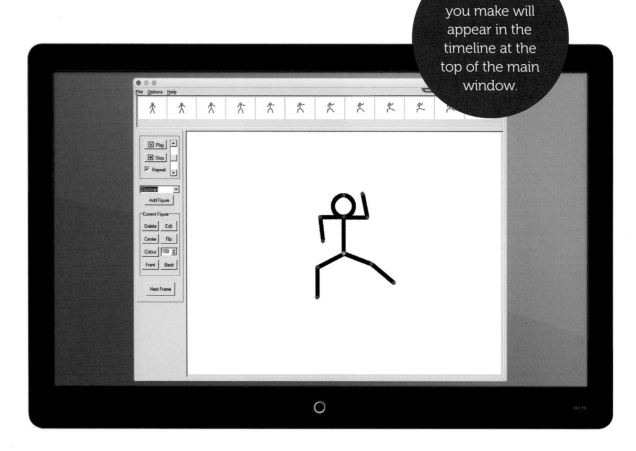

Add Another Stick Figure

Click the *Add Figure* button to make another stick figure. Use the buttons to flip it, make it thicker, or change the color.

Making Movie Magic

You can make a background for your animation. Check the *Options* screen to see what size the background needs to be.

Use the Paint program in Word to make a simple background. Then click the *Background* button in the menu to upload it. If you'd like, you can use a different background in different frames.

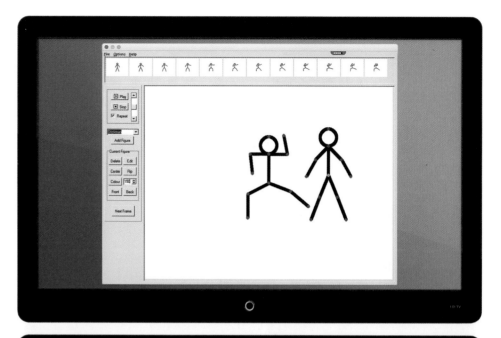

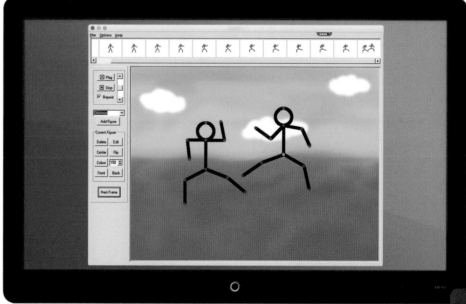

Short Videos

YOU WILL NEED:

- pencil
- paper
- scissors
- glue
- tablet or cell phone camera
- computer
- Animoto login (ask an adult)

Tip:

An adult can sign up for a free 14-day trial. Animoto also offers free accounts for educators.

MAKE A SHORT THIRTY-SECOND VIDEO.

Here's How:

1. Start with a blank sheet of paper. Make a mind map. Write your idea in the center. Circle it.

2. What do you want to show in thirty seconds? Draw a line. Write an action or an idea. Circle it.

3. Add more ideas and actions. Fill up the page.

4. Now it's time to choose. Cut out the circles. Move them around on the table. What will happen when? Add numbers to the circles. Now you have a storyboard.

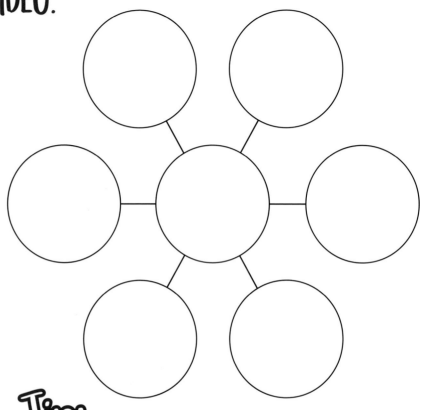

Tip:
You don't have to use all of the ideas on your mind map. Choose those you like best. Glue the numbered shot choices to a sheet of paper to make your storyboard.

5. Use your camera to photograph your choices.

6. Upload the images to a computer.

7. Ask an adult to open Animoto and sign in.

8. Choose a video style.

9. Select the music.

Tip:
To make a free video, click on the words, "Make a 30-second video for free."

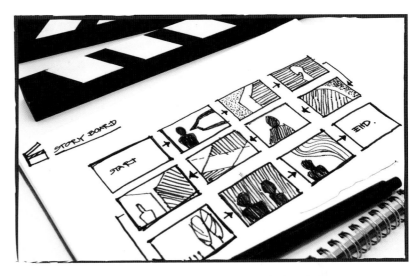

10. Add your pictures. Upload them from your computer.

11. Move the pictures in the correct order. Make the computer storyboard match your paper storyboard.

12. Add text to the pictures. Give the video a title.

Tip:

Movie directors always make a storyboard before they start filming. A storyboard helps the director plan the movie shot by shot.

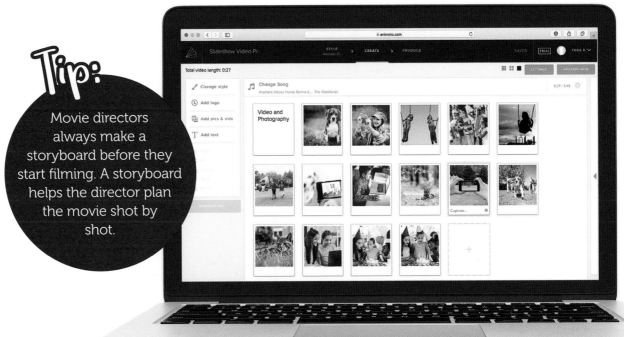

Editing Your Video

The first image will show for ten seconds. That is the **default** setting. If you keep that setting, you will only have time to show three images. Click on each image and use the slider to set the time you want.

The program will also let you edit your photographs. Your computer mouse can grab the corner and change the picture size. Does moving in closer make the picture look better? Or will a view from a distance better illustrate what you want to convey?

Making Movie Magic

When you edit an image in Animoto, a grid appears on top of the picture. The software is using the Rule of Thirds. It is using math to help you make unforgettable images.

The Rule of Thirds divides an image into thirds across and down. It makes a grid with nine rectangles.

How can you use it? Move the camera so the most important item is on or near these lines.

You can use the Rule of Thirds for long shots, mid-shots, and close-ups.

Stop-Motion Animation

YOU WILL NEED:

- paper
- pencil
- cell phone or tablet
- stop-motion animation app (ask an adult to download it)
- tripod (optional)
- items to move (plastic figures, Lego, cutouts, clay)

Tip:

If you have a webcam on a tripod, you can create stop-motion animation on a computer.

MAKE YOUR OWN ANIMATED MOVIE.

Here's How:

1. Begin with the story. Make a storyboard.

2. Create a stage for the actors. They need somewhere to move.

3. Add a tall background to the movie set. It can have one, two, or three sides.

Tip: You can build a set that looks like a real place. Or you can use a solid color for the set background.

4. Place an actor on the set.

5. Take the first picture. Stop the camera.

6. Move the actor a tiny bit. Take another picture. Stop the camera again.

7. Repeat the tiny movements. Take a picture of each one.

Tip:
If you use a tripod for the camera, it will hold the camera in the same place while you move the actor on the stage.

8. Now it's time to edit your movie. Add a title page.

9. Test different speeds.

10. Upload sound clips. Add special effects, like comic book words.

Making Movie Magic

Each stop-motion app has different editing tools. Experiment with each tool to see which effects you like best.

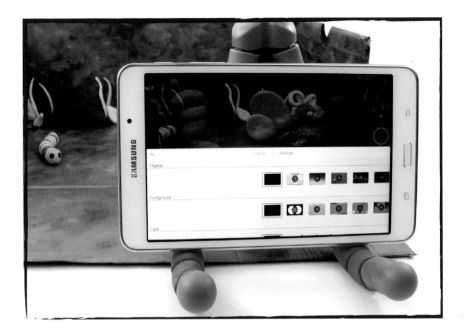

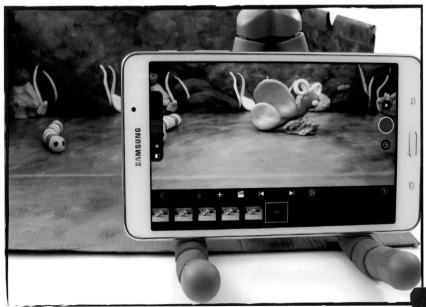

Green Screen

YOU WILL NEED:

- tablet or camera

- tripod

- green screen app (ask an adult to download it)

- green cloth or roll of paper

- step stool or ladder

- tall object to hang green screen over (curtain, pole, shelf)

- fasteners (clips, clothes pins, safety pins, duct tape, etc)

- large floor area to roll out green screen

- four lights

ADD COLORFUL BACKGROUNDS TO YOUR PHOTOS.

Here's How:

1. Hang a long green sheet up high.

2. Roll it out so it covers the wall and the floor.

3. Place the camera on a tripod in front of the green screen floor.

Tip:
Ask an adult to help you hang the back wall of the green sheet and fasten it.

4. Place two lights on each side of the green screen.

5. Point two lights at the back wall of the green screen.

6. Ask an actor to stand near the front of the green screen floor.

7. Point the two front lights at the actor.

Tip:
Twist the lights on each side at an angle so they don't cast shadows on the green screen or the actor. Place the front lights on each side of the camera.

8. Ask the actor to pose. Take a picture.

9. Import the photo into the green screen app.

10. Search for a good background picture online. Download it.

11. Import the background photo into the green screen app.

12. Follow the directions to combine the photo with the new background.

Making Movie Magic

You can add green screen backgrounds to movies, too. The software in the green screen app allows you to change the background for each new scene. Find some great backgrounds for your movie and start filming!

Glossary

animate (AN-uh-meyt): to show images one after another so an object appears to move

default (dih-FAWLT): the original instructions for a computer program

location (loh-KEY-shuhn): the place where something is

long shot (LONG shot): a camera shot taken at a great distance from a person

mid-shot (MID-shot): a camera shot taken at a medium distance from a person

stop-motion (stop-MOH-shuhn): a film that stops after each shot to move the object

Index

Show What You Know

1. Compare and contrast the three camera shots that movie directors use.

2. What size do you make the background for your stick figure animation?

3. Explain why movie directors use a storyboard.

4. How can a tripod help you film stop-action animation?

5. Why are four lights used to take shots with a green screen?

Websites to Visit

https://animoto.com/

www.commonsense.org/education/top-picks/websites-and-apps-for-making-videos-and-animation

http://pivotanimator.net/

About the Author

Anastasia Suen is the author of more than 250 books for young readers, including *Wired* (A Chicago Public Library Best of the Best Book) about how electricity flows from the power plant to your house. She reads, writes, and edits books in her studio in Northern California.

Meet The Author!
www.meetREMauthors.com

www.rourkeeducationalmedia.com

PHOTO CREDITS: Cover, Backcover, & Pages 5, 22–25: © creativelytara; Backcover: © kyoshino; Page 4: © SolStock, asiseeit, chuckcollier, GODS_AND_KINGS; Page 6: © SolStock, Page 7: © Manuel-F-O, RyanJLane, Lunja, chaofann; Page 8: © Kali9, Blackzheep; Page 9: © carrollphoto; Page 10: © kali9, stlee000; Page 11: © Wavebreakmedia; Page13: © Nastco; Page 16: © asiseeit; Page 18: © avdeev007, wabeno; Page 19: © Erdark; Page 20: © mixetto; Page 21: © vvvita, imagedepotpro, estherpoon; Page 26: © chuckcollier, GODS_AND_KINGS; Page 27: © Suljo; Page 28: © ilyarexi; Page 29: chuckcollier, sumroeng

Edited by: Keli Sipperley
Cover and Interior design by: Tara Raymo • CreativelyTara • www.creativelytara.com

Library of Congress PCN Data

Video Animation and Photography / Anastasia Suen
(Make It!)
ISBN 978-1-68342-381-2 (hard cover)
ISBN 978-1-68342-890-9 (soft cover)
ISBN 978-1-68342-547-2 (e-Book)
Library of Congress Control Number: 2017934543

Rourke Educational Media
Printed in the United States of America,
North Mankato, Minnesota